Breaking Free from Debt

C. P. Kumar
Reiki Healer
Roorkee - 247667, India

Disclaimer

While every effort has been made to ensure the accuracy and completeness of the content in this book, the author cannot guarantee that the information contained herein is error-free, up-to-date, or suitable for every individual circumstance.

The author shall not be held liable or responsible for any errors or omissions in the content of the book, nor for any damages, or losses that may arise from any actions taken based upon the suggestions or contents presented in the book.

Readers are advised to use their own judgment and discretion in applying the information provided in this book, and to consult with qualified professionals before taking any action based on the contents of this book. The author disclaims any and all liability or responsibility for any actions taken or not taken based on the information contained in this book.

DEDICATION

To all those who have felt the weight of financial burdens and dared to dream of a debt-free life.

To the resilient souls who embarked on a journey to break free from the chains of debt, armed with determination and a desire for financial freedom.

To the individuals who, with unwavering courage, confronted their debt demons and emerged victorious.

This book is dedicated to you. Your commitment to mastering the art of debt management and your unwavering spirit in the face of adversity serve as a beacon of hope for others striving to achieve financial independence.

May your stories inspire countless others to take control of their financial destinies, conquer their debts, and ultimately, embark on a path towards lasting prosperity.

C. P. Kumar

CONTENTS

PREFACE

In the turbulent sea of modern finance, the anchor of debt can weigh us down, holding us back from the shores of financial freedom. Whether it's the looming shadow of student loans, the unrelenting cycle of credit card debt, or the weighty responsibility of a mortgage, debt can dominate our lives. But it doesn't have to. This book, "Breaking Free from Debt", is your guide to liberation from the chains of financial burden.

Within these pages, you'll find a comprehensive roadmap to regain control of your financial destiny. From understanding the nature of debt to learning how to invest for your future, this book covers all aspects of the journey towards financial independence.

Debt is a formidable adversary, but with the right tools and strategies, you can conquer it. This book is your toolkit for that journey. It's designed to provide you with the knowledge, resources, and inspiration you need to embark on a path to financial emancipation.

Whether you're drowning in credit card debt or seeking ways to manage your mortgage, whether you're contemplating bankruptcy or planning your financial future, "Breaking Free from Debt" is here to guide you. We'll help you navigate through the complex terrain of debt management, providing you with practical advice, real-life examples, and expert insights every step of the way.

The stories of individuals who have successfully broken free from debt serve as beacons of hope and inspiration throughout the book. Their journeys from financial hardship to prosperity demonstrate that with determination, discipline, and the right strategies, anyone can overcome the shackles of debt.

So, if you're ready to embark on this transformative journey towards financial liberation, turn the page and let "Breaking Free from Debt" be your trusted companion. It's time to take control of your financial destiny and set sail towards a brighter, debt-free future.

C. P. Kumar
Reiki Healer
Former Scientist 'G', National Institute of Hydrology
Roorkee - 247667, India
Web: https://www.angelfire.com/nh/cpkumar/virgo.html

Introduction

In today's world, debt is an inescapable aspect of financial life for many individuals and organizations alike. Whether it's taking out a mortgage to purchase a home, securing a loan for higher education, or using credit cards for everyday expenses, debt is a financial tool that can help us achieve our goals. However, when not managed properly, debt can become a heavy burden, leading to financial stress and even bankruptcy. This article serves as an introduction to the vital concept of debt management, exploring what debt is, why managing it is crucial, and the common types of debt that people encounter in their lives.

Defining Debt

Before delving into the intricacies of debt management, it's essential to define what debt actually is. Debt is essentially a financial obligation or liability that arises when one party borrows money from another with the promise of repayment, often with interest, at a later date. This simple yet powerful concept forms the basis of many financial transactions in our modern world.

Debt can take various forms, including:

Consumer Debt: This type of debt encompasses personal loans, credit card balances, and other forms of borrowing for everyday expenses. Consumer debt is often unsecured, meaning it's not backed by collateral.

Mortgages: A mortgage is a secured loan used to purchase real estate. The property itself serves as collateral, and the loan is typically repaid over a long period, often decades.

Student Loans: These are loans specifically designed to help individuals finance their education. They may have lower interest rates and more flexible repayment terms than other types of debt.

Auto Loans: Borrowers take out auto loans to finance the purchase of a vehicle. Like mortgages, these loans are secured by the asset being purchased.

Business Loans: Companies often need capital to start, grow, or sustain their operations. Business loans can take various forms, including lines of credit, term loans, and equipment financing.

Debt Consolidation Loans: Some individuals choose to consolidate multiple high-interest debts into a single, lower-interest loan to simplify repayment.

The Importance of Debt Management

Now that we've defined debt let's explore why debt management is so crucial in the realm of personal finance and business operations.

Avoiding Financial Stress: Mismanaged debt can lead to overwhelming stress and anxiety. High-interest debt, in particular, can quickly spiral out of control, making it challenging to make timely payments. This can result in calls from creditors, late fees, and a constant feeling of financial pressure.

Maintaining Financial Stability: Effective debt management is essential for maintaining financial stability. By consistently making payments and reducing debt balances, individuals and businesses can build a solid financial foundation that allows for future growth and financial security.

Protecting Credit Scores: Your credit score is a crucial factor in obtaining favorable interest rates on loans, securing rental housing, and even getting hired for certain jobs. Debt management plays a vital role in maintaining a good credit score by ensuring that debts are paid on time and according to the agreed-upon terms.

Achieving Financial Goals: Managing debt wisely can help individuals and businesses achieve their financial goals. Whether it's saving for retirement, buying a home, or expanding a business, effective debt management can free up resources to invest in these objectives.

Avoiding Bankruptcy: In extreme cases, uncontrolled debt can lead to bankruptcy, which has serious and long-lasting consequences for individuals and businesses alike. Debt management strategies can help prevent this dire outcome by addressing financial challenges proactively.

Common Types of Debt

To gain a deeper understanding of debt management, it's essential to recognize the various types of debt individuals and organizations commonly encounter.

Credit Card Debt: Credit card debt refers to the outstanding balance that individuals owe on their credit cards when they have used them to make purchases or obtain cash advances. This debt accrues when cardholders do not pay their full credit card balance by the due date and are charged interest on the remaining amount. Credit card debt can become costly due to high-interest rates, and managing it effectively is essential to avoid financial strain and maintain a healthy financial status.

Credit cards can be incredibly convenient but can also lead to high-interest debt if not used responsibly. Managing credit card debt involves making timely payments, keeping balances low, and avoiding unnecessary fees.

Mortgage Debt: A mortgage is a type of loan used to finance the purchase of real estate, where the property itself serves as collateral for the loan, and the borrower makes regular payments to the lender over a specified period until the loan is fully repaid. If the borrower fails to make payments, the lender may have the right to take ownership of the property through a process known as foreclosure.

For most people, a mortgage is the largest debt they'll ever take on. Effective mortgage debt management involves choosing the right mortgage, making consistent payments, and exploring opportunities to refinance for better terms.

Student Loan Debt: Student loan debt is a type of financial obligation that individuals incur when they borrow money to pay for their education expenses, typically for higher education such as college or university. These loans are specifically designed to help students cover tuition, fees, books, and living expenses. Student loans often have favorable terms, such as lower interest rates and deferred payments while in school. However, they must be repaid, usually after the borrower graduates or leaves school, and can be a significant financial burden for many individuals.

Many individuals graduate from college with significant student loan debt. To manage this type of debt, borrowers can explore income-driven repayment plans, loan forgiveness programs, and strategies for accelerating repayment.

Auto Loan Debt: Auto loan debt refers to the money individuals borrow from a lender, such as a bank or a financial institution, to purchase a vehicle, usually a car or a truck. These loans come with an agreed-upon interest rate and repayment schedule. Borrowers make regular payments, often monthly, to pay off the loan over a set period. If the borrower fails to make payments as agreed, the lender may repossess the vehicle as collateral. Auto loan debt allows individuals to acquire a vehicle without paying the full purchase price upfront but involves paying interest on the borrowed amount.

Auto loans can be more manageable than some other types of debt due to the secured nature of the loan. However, it's still essential to make on-time payments and avoid financing options with high interest rates.

Business Debt: Business debt refers to the financial obligations that a company or business entity incurs when it borrows money to fund its operations, finance expansion, purchase assets, or meet other financial needs. This debt can take various forms, including loans, bonds, lines of credit, or trade credit from suppliers. Businesses typically use debt as a source of capital, and they are obligated to repay the borrowed funds, often with interest, according to the terms and conditions specified in the borrowing agreements. Managing business debt is crucial for maintaining financial stability and ensuring the company's long-term success.

Managing business debt involves careful financial planning, evaluating the return on investment for debt-funded projects, and maintaining a healthy debt-to-equity ratio. The debt-to-equity ratio is a financial metric that compares a company's total debt to its shareholders' equity, indicating the proportion of financing provided by creditors versus shareholders.

Debt Consolidation: Debt consolidation is a financial strategy in which an individual or organization combines multiple debts, such as credit card balances, loans, or other outstanding obligations, into a single, new loan or repayment plan. This is often done to simplify the debt repayment process, potentially reduce interest rates or monthly payments, and make it easier to manage and ultimately pay off the debt. Debt consolidation can be achieved through various methods, including taking out a consolidation loan, using a balance transfer credit card, or working with a debt consolidation company or counselor.

Personal Loans: Personal loans are unsecured loans that individuals can borrow from banks, credit unions, or online lenders for various personal financial needs. Unlike secured loans, such as auto or mortgage loans, personal loans do not require collateral. Borrowers receive a lump sum of money and agree to repay it, typically with interest, over a predetermined period, often ranging from a few months to several years. Personal loans can be used for a wide range of purposes, including consolidating debt, funding home improvements, covering medical expenses, or financing a vacation. The interest rates and terms of personal loans can vary based on the borrower's creditworthiness and the lender's policies. Managing personal loans involves understanding the terms, interest rates, and repayment schedule.

Conclusion

In the realm of personal finance and business operations, debt is a tool that, when managed effectively, can pave the way for achieving financial goals and maintaining stability. However, the improper management of debt can lead to financial stress, damaged credit, and even bankruptcy. Therefore, understanding the various types of debt and implementing sound debt management strategies are critical skills for individuals and organizations alike.

In the subsequent chapters of this book, we will delve deeper into the specifics of debt management, exploring practical tips and strategies for managing different types of debt and ultimately achieving financial freedom. Whether you're looking to eliminate credit card debt, navigate student loans, or make informed decisions about business debt, this book will equip you with the knowledge and tools you need to take control of your financial future and break free from the shackles of debt.

Introduction

Financial freedom is a goal that many of us aspire to achieve. It's about breaking free from the shackles of debt and living a life where you have control over your finances, rather than your finances controlling you. But before you can embark on the journey to financial freedom, you must first understand your current financial situation. This article will guide you through the process of assessing your financial health, creating a personal budget, and tracking your expenses, all of which are essential steps in breaking free from debt.

Assessing Your Current Financial Health

The first step in taking control of your finances is to assess your current financial health. This involves taking a close look at your income, expenses, assets, and liabilities. Here's how to get started:

Calculate Your Net Worth: Your net worth is a snapshot of your financial situation. To calculate it, add up the value of all your assets, including savings, investments, and the current market value of your home and vehicles. Next, subtract your liabilities, which include debts like credit card balances, loans, and mortgages. Your net worth is what remains, and it reflects your current financial standing. A positive net worth is a good sign, while a negative net worth indicates that you owe more than you own.

Review Your Income: Take a close look at your sources of income. Include your salary, any side hustles, rental income, and investment dividends. Understanding your income sources will help you plan your budget effectively.

Analyze Your Expenses: Track your monthly expenses meticulously. This includes fixed expenses like rent or mortgage payments, utilities, insurance premiums, and groceries, as well as variable expenses like dining out, entertainment, and discretionary spending. Be thorough and honest about where your money is going.

Identify Your Debts: Make a list of all your debts, including the outstanding balance, interest rates, and minimum monthly payments. This step is crucial, as it will help you prioritize which debts to tackle first.

Assess Your Financial Goals: Determine your short-term and long-term financial goals. These might include paying off credit card debt, saving for a down payment on a home, or building an emergency fund. Understanding your goals will guide your financial decisions.

Creating a Personal Budget

With a clear picture of your financial health, it's time to create a personal budget. A budget is a powerful tool that helps you allocate your income to cover your expenses and reach your financial goals. Here's how to create one:

Set Financial Goals: Based on your assessment of your financial health, establish clear and realistic financial goals. These goals will serve as the foundation for your budget.

Categorize Your Expenses: Divide your expenses into categories like housing, transportation, groceries, entertainment, and debt repayment. Categorization makes it easier to track and manage your spending.

Determine Fixed and Variable Expenses: Differentiate between fixed and variable expenses. Fixed expenses, like rent or mortgage payments, remain constant each month. Variable expenses, such as dining out or entertainment, can fluctuate.

Allocate Income to Categories: Start by covering your essential expenses like housing, utilities, groceries, and debt payments. Once those are accounted for, allocate funds to discretionary spending categories (non-essential or optional expenses). Be sure to allocate a portion of your income to savings and debt repayment.

Monitor Your Budget: A budget is a dynamic tool that requires ongoing attention. Regularly track your expenses and compare them to your budgeted amounts. This will help you stay on course and make adjustments if necessary.

Emergency Fund: Prioritize building an emergency fund as part of your budget. Having savings set aside for unexpected expenses can prevent you from relying on credit cards or loans in times of financial crisis.

Review and Adjust: Periodically review your budget to ensure it aligns with your financial goals. Life circumstances change, so your budget should evolve accordingly.

Tracking Expenses

Tracking your expenses is a crucial aspect of understanding and managing your financial situation. It's all too easy to overspend when you're not aware of where your money is going. Here's how to effectively track your expenses:

Choose a Tracking Method: Decide on a method for tracking your expenses. You can use a spreadsheet, a budgeting app, or even pen and paper. The key is to use a method that you're comfortable with and will stick to.

Record All Expenses: Make it a habit to record every single expense, no matter how small. This includes cash purchases, credit card transactions, and online payments. Don't let anything slip through the cracks.

Categorize Your Expenses: Categorize your expenses into the same categories you used in your budget. This will allow you to see which areas of your spending may need adjustment.

Set Spending Limits: As you track your expenses, compare them to your budgeted amounts. If you notice that you're consistently overspending in a particular category, adjust your budget or set stricter spending limits for that category.

Stay Disciplined: Tracking your expenses requires discipline and consistency. Make it a daily or weekly routine to update your expense tracker. The more diligent you are, the better insight you'll have into your spending habits.

Identify Patterns: Over time, you'll begin to notice spending patterns. These patterns can help you make informed decisions about where to cut back and where to allocate more funds.

Use Technology: Take advantage of budgeting apps and financial tools that can automate expense tracking and provide you with insights into your spending habits. Many apps also offer budgeting features to help you stay on track.

Conclusion

Understanding your financial situation is the foundation of achieving financial freedom and breaking free from debt. It's a process that involves assessing your current financial health, creating a personal budget, and tracking your expenses. By following these steps, you'll gain clarity about your financial strengths and weaknesses, allowing you to make informed decisions to improve your financial well-being.

Remember that financial freedom is a journey, and it requires dedication and discipline. But with a clear understanding of your financial situation and a well-structured plan, you can take control of your finances, pay off debt, and work toward a brighter financial future. So, take the first step today by assessing your financial health and setting achievable financial goals. Your path to financial freedom starts now.

Introduction

Debt is a ubiquitous aspect of modern life. Whether it's buying a home, financing education, or starting a business, many of us rely on loans to achieve our financial goals. However, not all debt is created equal. Some debts can be a stepping stone to prosperity, while others can become a crushing burden. In this article, we will delve into the world of good debt vs. bad debt, helping you understand how to make informed financial decisions and break free from the shackles of unsustainable debt.

Differentiating Between Productive and Non-Productive Debt

Before we can discuss the intricacies of good and bad debt, it's essential to establish a clear distinction between them.

Productive Debt

Productive debt, often referred to as "good debt," is an investment in your future financial well-being. It typically offers the potential for growth, income generation, or increased asset value. Here are some key characteristics of productive debt:

Investment in Assets: Productive debt is used to acquire assets that have the potential to appreciate or generate income over time. Examples include mortgages for real estate, student loans for education, and business loans to fund a startup.

Low-Interest Rates: Good debt often comes with lower interest rates, making it more affordable in the long run. Lenders see it as a less risky investment because it is backed by valuable assets or future earning potential.

Tax Benefits: In some cases, interest paid on productive debt can be tax-deductible, reducing the overall cost of borrowing. Mortgage interest, for example, may be tax-deductible, offering homeowners a financial advantage.

Positive Impact on Credit Score: Responsible management of productive debt can have a positive impact on your credit score. Timely payments and low credit utilization can boost your creditworthiness, which can be beneficial for future financial endeavors.

Non-Productive Debt

Non-productive debt, commonly known as "bad debt," is incurred for expenditures that do not contribute to your financial well-being or wealth creation. It often leads to financial strain and can be a significant obstacle to achieving your financial goals. Here are some characteristics of non-productive debt:

Consumer Purchases: Bad debt is often associated with consumer purchases like luxury items, vacations, or dining out. These expenditures do not generate income or appreciate in value.

High-Interest Rates: Non-productive debt typically comes with high-interest rates, which can result in substantial long-term costs. Credit card debt, payday loans, and personal loans are notorious for their exorbitant interest rates. Payday loans are short-term, high-interest loans typically requiring repayment on the borrower's next payday, often used by individuals facing immediate financial needs.

No Tax Benefits: Unlike productive debt, the interest on non-productive debt is usually not tax-deductible. This means you cannot offset the cost of borrowing with potential tax savings.

Negative Impact on Credit Score: Mismanagement of non-productive debt can lead to a lower credit score. Late payments, high credit utilization, and maxed-out credit cards (charged up to their maximum credit limits, leaving no available credit for further purchases) can all harm your creditworthiness.

Examples of Good and Bad Debt

Now that we understand the fundamental differences between good and bad debt, let's explore some real-life examples to illustrate these concepts further.

Examples of Good Debt

Mortgage: Taking out a mortgage to buy a home is often considered good debt. Homes tend to appreciate in value over time, and mortgage interest rates are typically lower than other forms of borrowing. Plus, homeownership provides stability and potential tax benefits.

Student Loans: Investing in education through student loans can be a wise decision. A college degree or vocational training can enhance your earning potential over your lifetime, making it an investment in your future income.

Business Loans: Entrepreneurs often rely on business loans to fund their ventures. When used wisely, these loans can lead to business growth and increased profitability, ultimately paying off the debt and generating income.

Examples of Bad Debt

Credit Card Debt: Credit cards can be a convenient payment method, but carrying a balance and paying only the minimum amount due can lead to high-interest debt. Purchasing non-essential items with credit cards can quickly spiral into a financial crisis.

Payday Loans: Payday loans, with their astronomical interest rates, are a prime example of bad debt. These loans target individuals in urgent need of cash but can trap them in a cycle of debt due to their high costs.

Auto Loans for Depreciating Assets: Financing a brand-new car can be tempting, but cars are depreciating assets. Borrowing money for a rapidly depreciating item means you'll owe more than the car is worth, often leading to financial loss.

Strategies for Minimizing Bad Debt

Now that you can distinguish between good and bad debt, it's crucial to develop strategies to minimize or eliminate the latter from your financial life. Here are some effective approaches to help you break free from bad debt:

Budgeting and Financial Planning: Create a detailed budget that accounts for all your income and expenses. This will help you identify areas where you can cut unnecessary spending and redirect those funds towards paying down debt.

Emergency Fund: **Build an emergency fund to cover** unexpected expenses. Having a financial cushion can prevent you from turning to high-interest loans when unexpected bills arise.

Debt Snowball or Debt Avalanche: **Choose a debt** repayment strategy that works for you. The debt snowball method focuses on paying off the smallest debt first, providing a psychological boost, while the debt avalanche method tackles the highest-interest debt first, saving you money in the long run.

Consolidation Loans: **If you have multiple high-interest** debts, consider consolidating them into a single loan with a lower interest rate. This can make repayment more manageable and cost-effective.

Lifestyle Adjustments: **Temporarily adjust your lifestyle to** free up more money for debt repayment. This might mean cooking at home more often, canceling subscription services, or finding less expensive ways to entertain yourself.

Increase Income: **Explore opportunities to boost your** income, such as taking on a part-time job, freelancing, or monetizing a hobby. The extra income can be dedicated to paying down debt faster.

Seek Professional Help: **If your debt situation is** overwhelming, don't hesitate to seek assistance from a credit counseling agency or a financial advisor. They can provide guidance and help you create a realistic plan to tackle your debt.

Conclusion

In the journey to financial freedom, understanding the distinction between good debt and bad debt is crucial. Good debt can serve as a valuable tool for achieving your financial goals, while bad debt can derail your progress and lead to financial hardship. By making informed decisions, budgeting wisely, and implementing effective debt reduction strategies, you can break free from the burden of unsustainable debt and pave the way to a more secure and prosperous financial future. Remember, the path to financial freedom begins with the choices you make today.

Introduction

Debt is a financial burden that many individuals and households face at some point in their lives. While it's often seen as a necessary part of achieving certain goals, such as homeownership or higher education, it can also become a daunting obstacle if not managed wisely. In this article, we will delve into the various types of debt that individuals encounter on their financial journeys, exploring the unique characteristics and considerations associated with each. By gaining a better understanding of these different forms of debt, you can make informed decisions to break free from its grasp and secure a more stable financial future.

Credit Card Debt

Credit card debt is one of the most common and pervasive forms of debt in modern society. It typically arises when individuals use credit cards to make purchases but fail to pay off the full balance by the due date, incurring interest charges. Credit cards offer convenience and flexibility, but if not managed responsibly, they can lead to a cycle of debt that's challenging to escape.

The key to managing credit card debt is to stay disciplined with your spending and pay off the balance in full each month to avoid interest charges. If you're already in credit card debt, consider creating a repayment plan, prioritizing higher-interest cards first. Additionally, exploring balance transfer options with lower interest rates can be a strategic move to reduce your debt burden.

Student Loans

Higher education can be a pathway to a better future, but it often comes with a hefty price tag. Student loans are designed to help individuals cover the costs of college or vocational training, with the expectation that they will be repaid after graduation. There are federal and private student loans, each with its own terms and conditions.

Federal student loans typically offer more favorable interest rates and flexible repayment options compared to private loans. Income-driven repayment plans, loan forgiveness programs, and deferment or forbearance options are available to provide relief for borrowers facing financial hardships. It's crucial to research and understand the terms of your student loans and explore the options available to you to manage this type of debt effectively.

Mortgages

For many people, owning a home is a lifelong dream, and mortgages make that dream a reality. A mortgage is a long-term loan used to finance the purchase of a home. Unlike other forms of debt, a mortgage is secured by the property itself, which means the lender can foreclose on the home if the borrower fails to make payments.

When considering a mortgage, it's essential to shop around for the best interest rates and loan terms. A down payment can significantly impact the overall cost of your mortgage, so saving for a substantial down payment is advisable. Additionally, understanding the different types of mortgages, such as fixed-rate and adjustable-rate mortgages, can help you choose the one that best fits your financial situation and goals.

Auto Loans

Auto loans are a common way to finance the purchase of a car. These loans can be obtained from banks, credit unions, or dealerships, and they come in various forms, including traditional loans and leases. Auto loans are typically secured by the vehicle itself, making them a secured form of debt.

When taking out an auto loan, consider factors such as the loan term, interest rate, and down payment. Longer loan terms may offer lower monthly payments but result in higher overall interest costs. It's essential to strike a balance that aligns with your budget and financial goals. Additionally, be cautious of add-on products and extended warranties that can inflate the cost of your loan.

Personal Loans

Personal loans are unsecured loans that individuals can use for various purposes, such as debt consolidation, home improvements, or unexpected expenses. Unlike secured loans, personal loans do not require collateral, making them a popular choice for borrowers with good credit.

Interest rates on personal loans can vary widely based on your creditworthiness and the lender's policies. It's crucial to compare offers from multiple lenders to secure the best terms and rates. Personal loans can be a useful tool for managing debt or pursuing important financial goals, but it's essential to use them wisely and avoid taking on unnecessary debt.

Medical Debt

Medical debt is an unfortunate consequence of unexpected healthcare expenses. Even with health insurance, many individuals and families find themselves facing substantial medical bills that can be difficult to manage. Medical debt often results from co-pays, deductibles, and out-of-network costs.

If you're struggling with medical debt, it's essential to communicate with healthcare providers and insurance companies to understand your options. Many providers offer payment plans or financial assistance programs to help patients manage their bills. Additionally, consider budgeting for potential medical expenses and exploring health savings accounts (HSAs) or flexible spending accounts (FSAs) to mitigate the impact of medical debt on your finances.

An HSA is a tax-advantaged savings account for individuals with high-deductible health plans, allowing them to save money for medical expenses with tax benefits. An FSA is a tax-advantaged account offered by employers that enables employees to set aside pre-tax dollars to cover eligible medical expenses incurred during the plan year.

Conclusion

Debt is a financial reality for most people, but it doesn't have to be a lifelong burden. Understanding the various types of debt and how they work is the first step toward breaking free from its grip. Whether you're dealing with credit card debt, student loans, mortgages, auto loans, personal loans, or medical debt, there are strategies and resources available to help you regain control of your finances.

The key to successful debt management is responsible financial planning and decision-making. Create a budget, prioritize high-interest debt, explore consolidation options, and seek professional advice if needed. Remember that breaking free from debt is a journey that requires patience and discipline, but with the right approach, you can achieve financial freedom and secure a more stable future for yourself and your family.

Introduction

Debt is a common aspect of modern life, with many people finding themselves burdened by various forms of financial obligations. Managing multiple debts can be overwhelming and can lead to financial stress and instability. Fortunately, there are strategies to help individuals regain control of their finances and work towards a debt-free future. Two such strategies are debt consolidation and refinancing.

In this article, we will delve into the world of debt consolidation and refinancing, exploring the key differences between these approaches, their respective advantages and disadvantages, and how to determine which one is the right choice for your unique financial situation. By the end, you'll have a clearer understanding of these financial tools and be better equipped to make informed decisions on your path to financial freedom.

Consolidation vs. Refinancing: Understanding the Difference

Debt Consolidation

Debt consolidation is a financial strategy that involves combining multiple existing debts into a single, more manageable loan. The idea behind debt consolidation is to simplify your financial obligations, making it easier to keep track of payments and potentially reduce the overall cost of your debt.

Key aspects of debt consolidation:

Single Payment: **By consolidating your debts, you can streamline your monthly payments into a single, more manageable payment. This can help prevent missed payments and late fees, which can negatively impact your credit score.**

Lower Interest Rate: **In some cases, debt consolidation may allow you to secure a lower interest rate on the new consolidated loan compared to the interest rates on your existing debts. This can result in significant savings over time.**

Extended Repayment Terms: **Debt consolidation loans often come with longer repayment terms, which can reduce the monthly payment amount. While this can provide immediate relief, it may also mean paying more in interest over the life of the loan.**

Secured vs. Unsecured: **Debt consolidation loans can be either secured or unsecured. Secured loans are backed by collateral, such as your home or a valuable asset, while unsecured loans are not tied to any collateral. Secured loans typically offer lower interest rates but carry the risk of losing the collateral if you default on the loan.**

Refinancing

Refinancing, on the other hand, involves replacing an existing loan with a new loan that has different terms, often with the goal of securing better terms, such as a lower interest rate or a shorter repayment period. While debt consolidation primarily focuses on simplifying your debt structure, refinancing aims to optimize the terms of your existing loans.

Key aspects of refinancing:

Lower Interest Rate: One of the primary reasons people choose to refinance is to obtain a lower interest rate on their existing loans. A lower rate can result in reduced monthly payments and less interest paid over the life of the loan.

Change in Loan Term: Refinancing allows you to change the length of your loan term. For example, you can refinance a 30-year mortgage into a 15-year mortgage, which may increase your monthly payments but help you pay off the loan faster and save on interest.

Cash-Out Refinance: In some cases, homeowners with equity in their properties may choose a cash-out refinance, where they borrow more than the current loan balance and receive the difference in cash. This can be used for various purposes, including debt consolidation, home improvements, or investments.

Improved Loan Terms: Refinancing can also help you switch from adjustable-rate mortgages to fixed-rate mortgages or vice versa, depending on your financial goals and risk tolerance.

Pros and Cons of Debt Consolidation and Refinancing

Debt Consolidation Pros:

Simplified Payments: The most significant advantage of debt consolidation is simplifying your financial life by combining multiple debts into one. This reduces the risk of missing payments and incurring late fees.

Lower Interest Rates: **If you can secure a lower interest rate on your consolidated loan, you can save money over time and pay off your debt more efficiently.**

Potential for Better Terms: **Debt consolidation may offer more favorable loan terms, such as longer repayment periods, which can reduce your monthly payments.**

Debt Consolidation Cons:

Extended Repayment: **While lower monthly payments may offer immediate relief, longer repayment terms can result in paying more interest over the life of the loan.**

Secured Loans: **Opting for a secured consolidation loan puts your assets at risk if you fail to make payments, potentially jeopardizing your home or other valuable possessions.**

Refinancing Pros:

Lower Interest Rates: **Refinancing often leads to lower interest rates, which can significantly reduce the overall cost of your debt.**

Flexible Loan Terms: **You can choose loan terms that better align with your financial goals, whether that means shorter terms for faster debt repayment or longer terms for lower monthly payments.**

Cash-Out Option: **Homeowners may access their home's equity through a cash-out refinance, providing funds for debt consolidation or other financial needs.**

Refinancing Cons:

Closing Costs: Refinancing typically involves closing costs, which can add to the upfront cost of the new loan. It's essential to calculate whether the potential savings over time outweigh these costs.

Risk of Overborrowing: Accessing home equity through a cash-out refinance can lead to overborrowing, increasing your debt burden if not managed wisely.

How to Choose the Right Option

Choosing between debt consolidation and refinancing depends on your financial goals, current situation, and the types of debt you hold. Here are some factors to consider when deciding which option is right for you:

Types of Debt: Assess the types of debt you have. Debt consolidation is suitable for unsecured debts like credit card debt and personal loans. Refinancing, especially mortgage refinancing, is ideal for secured debts like home loans.

Interest Rates: Compare the interest rates on your existing debts with the rates offered for debt consolidation or refinancing. If you can secure a significantly lower interest rate, it may make sense to pursue that option.

Monthly Payment Affordability: Consider your budget and how much you can afford to pay each month. Debt consolidation may offer lower monthly payments, while refinancing can be used to shorten the repayment term and pay off debt faster.

Credit Score: Your credit score plays a crucial role in the interest rates and terms you can qualify for. Debt consolidation may be more accessible for individuals with good credit, while refinancing may require higher creditworthiness, especially for mortgage refinancing.

Collateral: Think about whether you are comfortable putting up collateral for a debt consolidation loan. If you're hesitant to risk your assets, you might lean more towards refinancing.

Long-Term vs. Short-Term Goals: Consider your long-term financial goals. If your aim is to pay off debt quickly and save on interest, refinancing with a shorter term might be the right choice. Debt consolidation may be a better option if you need immediate relief and prefer lower monthly payments.

Closing Costs and Fees: If you're considering refinancing, be sure to factor in closing costs and fees associated with the new loan. These upfront costs can affect the overall cost savings.

Consultation with a Financial Advisor: When in doubt, seek advice from a financial advisor or credit counselor. They can provide personalized guidance based on your specific financial situation.

Conclusion

Dealing with debt can be a daunting task, but debt consolidation and refinancing are powerful tools that can help you regain control of your financial future. Each approach has its unique benefits and drawbacks, making it essential to carefully evaluate your circumstances and goals before making a decision.

Debt consolidation simplifies your financial life by combining multiple debts into one, potentially lowering your interest rates and offering more manageable monthly payments. On the other hand, refinancing allows you to optimize the terms of your existing loans, securing lower interest rates and tailoring your repayment schedule to align with your financial objectives.

Ultimately, the right choice between debt consolidation and refinancing depends on your specific financial situation, the types of debts you hold, your creditworthiness, and your long-term financial goals. By understanding the key differences between these two strategies and considering the pros and cons, you can make an informed decision that sets you on the path to breaking free from debt and achieving financial stability.

Introduction

Debt can be a heavy burden that weighs down on your financial well-being and overall quality of life. Whether you're dealing with credit card debt, student loans, or any other form of financial obligation, finding the right debt repayment strategy is crucial to achieving financial freedom. This article will explore some effective debt repayment strategies that can help you regain control of your finances and pave the way for a debt-free future.

The Snowball Method

The Snowball Method is a debt repayment strategy popularized by financial expert Dave Ramsey. This approach is designed to provide a psychological boost by targeting your smallest debts first, regardless of their interest rates. Here's how it works:

List Your Debts: Start by creating a comprehensive list of all your debts, from the smallest balance to the largest.

Minimum Payments: Continue making the minimum payments on all your debts to avoid late fees and penalties.

Focus on the Smallest Debt: Allocate any extra funds you can to the smallest debt on your list while making minimum payments on the others. This debt becomes your primary target.

Celebrate Small Victories: As you pay off your smallest debts, you'll experience a sense of accomplishment. Celebrate these victories to stay motivated.

Roll Over Payments: Once you've paid off a debt, take the money you were putting towards it (minimum payment plus any extra) and apply it to the next smallest debt on your list.

Repeat the Process: Continue this process until all your debts are paid off.

The Snowball Method is effective because it provides quick wins, boosting your confidence and motivation as you work towards larger debts. While it may not save you as much money on interest as some other methods, its psychological benefits can make it a valuable strategy for many.

The Avalanche Method

The Avalanche Method, also known as the Debt Stacking Method, takes a different approach by targeting the debts with the highest interest rates first. While it may not provide the same immediate psychological boost as the Snowball Method, it can save you more money on interest in the long run. Here's how it works:

List Your Debts: Similar to the Snowball Method, create a list of all your debts, but this time, order them from highest to lowest interest rate.

Minimum Payments: Continue making the minimum payments on all your debts.

Focus on the Highest Interest Debt: Allocate any extra funds you have to the debt with the highest interest rate. This debt becomes your primary target.

Snowball Effect: As you pay off the high-interest debts, you'll free up more money to put towards the next highest interest debt.

Repeat the Process: Continue this process until all your debts are paid off.

The Avalanche Method is financially efficient because it minimizes the amount you spend on interest payments over time. It's a particularly suitable strategy for those who are motivated by the prospect of saving money on interest and are willing to stay the course even without immediate victories.

Debt Repayment Apps and Tools

In today's digital age, there's a wealth of technology-driven tools and apps designed to assist you in managing and paying off your debts more effectively. Here are some popular ones:

Debt Payoff Planner Apps: Apps like Tally and Qoins help you create a personalized debt repayment plan based on your financial situation. They also automate payments and provide progress tracking.

Budgeting Apps: Tools like YNAB (You Need a Budget) and Mint allow you to create budgets, set financial goals, and track your debt repayment progress in real-time.

Debt Consolidation Loans: Platforms like SoFi and LendingClub offer debt consolidation loans that can simplify your debt repayment by combining multiple debts into a single, lower-interest loan.

Credit Score Monitoring Apps: Monitoring your credit score is essential during debt repayment. Apps like Credit Karma and Credit Sesame offer free credit score tracking and financial advice.

Financial Literacy Resources: Websites and apps like NerdWallet and Credit.com provide educational resources, calculators, and tools to help you make informed financial decisions.

Payment Reminder Apps: If you struggle with remembering due dates, apps like Prism and BillMinder can send you reminders and help you avoid late fees.

Conclusion

Breaking free from debt is a journey that requires dedication, discipline, and the right strategy. Whether you choose the Snowball Method to gain quick wins or the Avalanche Method to save on interest in the long term, the most important thing is to start. Use the debt repayment apps and tools available to your advantage, and don't hesitate to seek professional advice if needed.

Remember that debt repayment is not just about managing your finances; it's also about cultivating healthy financial habits that will serve you well throughout your life. By taking control of your debt and making consistent efforts to pay it off, you can achieve financial freedom and pave the way for a brighter financial future.

Introduction

Debt can be a heavy burden, causing stress and anxiety that affects every aspect of your life. If you're struggling to meet your financial obligations and feel overwhelmed by debt, you're not alone. Many people find themselves in a similar situation at some point in their lives. The good news is that there are ways to regain control of your finances and work towards a debt-free future. One powerful tool in your debt management arsenal is negotiating with your creditors.

Negotiating with creditors involves reaching out to the institutions or individuals to whom you owe money and discussing alternative arrangements that can make your debt more manageable. In this article, we will explore the key aspects of negotiating with creditors as part of your journey to break free from debt.

How to Contact Creditors

Before you can begin negotiating with your creditors, you need to establish clear lines of communication. Here are some steps to help you get started:

Gather Information: Begin by collecting all the necessary information about your debts. This includes the names of your creditors, the outstanding balances, interest rates, and any other relevant details. Having this information at your fingertips will be crucial during negotiations.

Compile Your Budget: Take the time to create a comprehensive budget that outlines your income and expenses. This will help you determine how much you can realistically allocate to debt repayment each month.

Identify Your Preferred Method of Communication: Decide whether you prefer to communicate with creditors through phone calls, emails, or written letters. Each method has its advantages, but it's essential to choose the one that you are most comfortable with.

Open Lines of Communication: Reach out to your creditors and inform them of your intention to negotiate. Explain your financial situation honestly, highlighting any significant changes that have affected your ability to meet your obligations.

Negotiating Lower Interest Rates

One of the most effective ways to make your debt more manageable is by negotiating lower interest rates with your creditors. High-interest rates can significantly increase the amount you owe over time, so reducing them can be a game-changer. Here's how you can approach this negotiation:

Understand Your Current Rates: Before contacting your creditors, make sure you fully understand the interest rates you are currently paying on your debts. This will serve as a reference point during negotiations.

Research Comparable Rates: Look up current interest rates for similar financial products, such as credit cards or loans. This will give you a basis for comparison when discussing lower rates with your creditors.

Prepare Your Case: Develop a compelling case for why you deserve a lower interest rate. This could include your history of on-time payments, loyalty as a customer, or financial hardship that justifies a reduction.

Contact Your Creditors: Reach out to your creditors and express your desire to lower your interest rates. Be polite and respectful during these conversations. Explain your reasons for requesting a lower rate and provide any supporting documentation if necessary.

Be Persistent: Don't be discouraged if your initial request is denied. Sometimes, you may need to speak with multiple representatives or escalate the matter to a supervisor. Persistence can pay off in the form of reduced interest rates.

Setting Up Repayment Plans

Negotiating lower interest rates is just one aspect of dealing with creditors. In many cases, you'll also need to work out a repayment plan that fits your financial situation. Here's how to go about it:

Assess Your Financial Capacity: Based on your budget and income, determine how much you can reasonably afford to pay towards your debts each month. Be realistic about what you can manage without compromising your essential living expenses.

Prioritize Debts: Not all debts are equal. Some may have higher interest rates or more severe consequences for non-payment. Prioritize your debts based on these factors and allocate more funds to those that are most urgent.

Contact Creditors with a Proposal: Reach out to each creditor with a proposed repayment plan. Be specific about the amount you can pay, the frequency of payments (e.g., monthly or bi-weekly), and the duration of the plan. Explain how this plan will help you become debt-free.

Negotiate with Flexibility: Creditors may not always agree to your proposed plan as-is. Be open to negotiation and compromise. They may suggest adjustments that can still help you reach your goal.

Get It in Writing: Once you and your creditor agree on a repayment plan, ensure that all terms are documented in writing. This serves as a legally binding agreement and protects both parties.

Conclusion

Negotiating with creditors is a crucial step in the journey to break free from debt. By establishing communication with your creditors, negotiating lower interest rates, and setting up reasonable repayment plans, you can take control of your financial situation and work towards a debt-free future.

Remember that the key to successful negotiations with creditors is honesty, persistence, and a clear understanding of your financial capabilities. Don't be afraid to seek professional help or credit counseling if you find the process overwhelming.

Breaking free from debt is a challenging but achievable goal, and negotiating with creditors is a valuable tool to help you get there. By taking proactive steps to address your debts, you can pave the way for a brighter and more financially stable future.

Introduction

In today's financial landscape, your credit score and credit report wield a significant influence over your ability to access credit, secure loans, and even determine the interest rates you're offered. Whether you're striving to break free from debt or simply seeking financial stability, understanding the intricacies of your credit score and credit report is paramount. This article will delve into the fundamentals of credit scoring, the importance of monitoring your credit report, strategies for improving your credit score, and conclude with insights into how this knowledge can empower you on your journey to financial freedom.

Understanding Your Credit Score

Your credit score, often referred to as a FICO score, is a three-digit number that encapsulates your creditworthiness. It's a numerical representation of your credit history, which lenders utilize to assess the risk of lending to you. Here are some key components of understanding your credit score:

1. Credit Score Factors

Your credit score is calculated using several factors, including your payment history, credit utilization, length of credit history, types of credit, and recent credit inquiries. Each of these components carries a different weight in determining your score.

2. Credit Score Range

Credit scores typically range from 300 to 850, with higher scores indicating better creditworthiness. A score above 700 is generally considered good, while a score below 600 may be seen as a sign of credit risk.

3. Payment History

Your payment history is one of the most significant factors affecting your credit score. Timely payments of bills and loans positively impact your score, while late or missed payments can have a detrimental effect.

4. Credit Utilization

Credit utilization reflects the amount of available credit you're using. High credit card balances relative to your credit limit can lower your score. It's advisable to keep your credit utilization below 30% to maintain a healthy score.

Monitoring Your Credit Report

Regularly monitoring your credit report is essential for maintaining financial health and safeguarding against identity theft. Your credit report is a detailed record of your credit history, including credit accounts, payment history, and public records. Here's what you should know about credit report monitoring:

1. Annual Free Credit Reports

By law, you are entitled to a free credit report from each of the three major credit bureaus (United States) - Experian, Equifax, and TransUnion - once a year. Take advantage of this opportunity to review your credit reports for inaccuracies or discrepancies.

Obtaining a credit report in a country other than the United States typically involves contacting the credit reporting agencies or bureaus that operate in that specific country. The process can vary from one country to another, but here are some general steps to obtain a credit report in most countries:

Identify the Credit Bureaus: Determine which credit reporting agencies or bureaus operate in the country where you want to obtain your credit report. These bureaus may have different names in different countries.

Contact the Credit Bureaus: Once you have identified the relevant credit bureaus, visit their websites or contact them directly to understand their procedures for obtaining a credit report. Look for information on how to request your credit report.

Provide Required Information: Be prepared to provide personal information and documentation to verify your identity. This may include your full name, date of birth, address history, and possibly a copy of your identification.

Request the Credit Report: Follow the instructions provided by the credit bureau to formally request your credit report. Some countries may allow you to request your report online, while others may require you to make the request by mail or in person.

Pay Any Applicable Fees: In some countries, there may be fees associated with obtaining your credit report. Make sure to inquire about any fees and arrange for payment if necessary.

Wait for Processing: Credit bureaus typically take some time to process your request and provide you with your credit report. The processing time can vary depending on the country and the bureau.

Review Your Credit Report: Once you receive your credit report, carefully review it for accuracy. Check for any errors, discrepancies, or unfamiliar accounts.

Dispute Errors: If you find inaccuracies in your credit report, follow the credit bureau's procedures for disputing and correcting errors.

It's important to note that the availability of credit reports, the procedures for obtaining them, and the regulations governing credit reporting can vary significantly from one country to another. Therefore, it's essential to research and follow the specific guidelines and requirements for the country in question. Additionally, some countries may not have well-established credit reporting systems, making it challenging to obtain a formal credit report in the same way you would in countries with more developed financial infrastructure.

2. Checking for Errors

Mistakes can occur on credit reports, and these errors can negatively impact your credit score. Common errors include incorrect personal information, duplicate accounts, or fraudulent activity. Dispute any inaccuracies promptly with the credit bureau.

Consider using credit monitoring services or apps that provide real-time updates on changes to your credit report. These services can alert you to suspicious activity or unexpected drops in your credit score.

4. Identity Theft Protection

Monitoring your credit report also serves as an effective tool against identity theft. By regularly reviewing your report, you can quickly spot any unauthorized accounts or credit inquiries.

Improving Your Credit Score

If your credit score isn't where you'd like it to be, there are proactive steps you can take to improve it. Improving your credit score is a gradual process, but the long-term benefits are worth the effort. Here are some strategies to consider:

1. Pay Your Bills On Time

Consistently making on-time payments is the most effective way to boost your credit score. Set up reminders or automatic payments to ensure you never miss a due date.

2. Reduce Credit Card Balances

High credit card balances relative to your credit limit can negatively affect your score. Focus on paying down outstanding balances to lower your credit utilization ratio.

3. Avoid Opening Too Many New Accounts

Each credit inquiry can temporarily lower your credit score. Be selective about opening new credit accounts, and only apply for credit when necessary.

4. Maintain Older Accounts

The length of your credit history matters. Keep older accounts open, even if you don't use them regularly, to demonstrate a longer credit history.

5. Diversify Your Credit Mix

A mix of different types of credit, such as credit cards, installment loans, and retail accounts, can positively impact your credit score. However, only open new credit accounts if it aligns with your financial goals.

6. Address Negative Items

If you have negative items on your credit report, such as late payments or collections, consider negotiating with creditors or working with credit repair professionals to address and resolve these issues.

Conclusion

Your credit score and credit report are pivotal tools in your quest to break free from debt and achieve financial stability. Understanding how credit scoring works, regularly monitoring your credit report for accuracy and security, and proactively taking steps to improve your credit score are all essential elements of financial success.

Remember that building and maintaining good credit is a journey, not a sprint. It requires discipline, patience, and a commitment to responsible financial practices. By taking control of your credit and staying informed, you can pave the way to a brighter financial future, one where you have the freedom to make the most of your financial resources while avoiding the burdens of excessive debt.

Introduction

In today's financially complex world, many individuals and businesses find themselves grappling with overwhelming debt. The burden of debt can be emotionally and financially taxing, leading many to seek relief through bankruptcy or other debt relief options. This article delves into the intricacies of bankruptcy and explores alternative debt relief solutions, shedding light on the factors to consider and the processes involved. By the end of this article, you'll have a comprehensive understanding of the choices available for breaking free from debt.

When to Consider Bankruptcy

Bankruptcy is a legal process that allows individuals and businesses to discharge or restructure their debts when they are unable to meet their financial obligations. However, bankruptcy should not be viewed as a quick fix for every financial challenge. There are specific situations in which considering bankruptcy may be the most viable option:

Overwhelming Debt: When your debt load becomes unmanageable, and your income cannot keep up with your financial obligations, bankruptcy may offer a way out. This typically occurs when your debt-to-income ratio is too high to sustain.

Foreclosure or Repossession: Foreclosure or repossession is the legal process by which a lender seizes and takes ownership of a property or asset when the borrower defaults on loan payments. If you're at risk of losing your home due to foreclosure or other assets due to repossession, bankruptcy can provide an automatic stay, temporarily halting these proceedings and giving you time to reevaluate your financial situation.

Mounting Medical Bills: Sudden illness or injury can lead to sky-high medical bills, causing significant financial strain. Bankruptcy can help discharge medical debts, providing a fresh start for individuals facing this challenge.

Unemployment or Reduced Income: When a job loss or a significant decrease in income disrupts your financial stability, bankruptcy can be a lifeline to help you regain control of your finances.

Constant Harassment by Creditors: If creditors and collection agencies are incessantly hounding you with calls and threats, bankruptcy can put an end to this harassment through an automatic stay.

Legal Actions: Facing lawsuits, wage garnishments, or other legal actions due to unpaid debts may necessitate bankruptcy as a strategic financial move to protect your assets.

One significant disadvantage of bankruptcy is the negative impact it has on your creditworthiness, making it difficult to access credit, secure loans, or obtain favorable interest rates in the future. Additionally, bankruptcy can result in the loss of assets and may not discharge all types of debts, such as student loans or child support payments. It can also have long-term financial and personal consequences, including a tarnished financial reputation and potential difficulties in securing housing or employment.

Alternative Debt Relief Solutions

While bankruptcy is a powerful tool for debt relief, it's not the only option available. It's important to explore alternative solutions before committing to bankruptcy, as it can have long-lasting implications on your credit and financial future. Here are some alternative debt relief options to consider:

Debt Consolidation: Debt consolidation involves taking out a single loan to pay off multiple debts. This simplifies your monthly payments and may result in a lower interest rate, making it easier to manage your debt.

Debt Management Plans (DMPs): Non-profit credit counseling agencies can help you create a DMP. This plan involves negotiating with creditors for lower interest rates and more favorable terms, allowing you to repay your debts over a structured period.

Debt Settlement: Debt settlement involves negotiating with creditors to settle your debts for less than the full amount owed. While this can provide debt relief, it can also negatively impact your credit score and may involve tax consequences.

Budgeting and Financial Counseling: Sometimes, a simple adjustment to your budget and financial habits can help you regain control of your finances. Financial counseling services can provide guidance on managing your money more effectively.

Home Equity Loans or Lines of Credit: A home equity loan is a type of loan that allows homeowners to borrow money using their home's equity as collateral, typically with a fixed interest rate and structured repayment plan. A line of credit is a flexible borrowing arrangement that allows individuals or businesses to access funds up to a predetermined limit and repay, reuse, or carry a balance as needed, with interest typically charged only on the amount borrowed.

If you own a home and have built up equity, you may consider using a home equity loan or line of credit to consolidate or pay off high-interest debts. However, this option carries the risk of losing your home if you cannot make the payments.

Negotiating with Creditors: In some cases, you may be able to negotiate directly with creditors for better repayment terms, such as reduced interest rates, lower monthly payments, or extended repayment periods.

The Bankruptcy Process

If you've determined that bankruptcy is the most appropriate debt relief option for your situation, it's crucial to understand the bankruptcy process thoroughly. Bankruptcy law in the United States primarily revolves around two main types of bankruptcy. Chapter 7 and Chapter 13 of the United States Bankruptcy Code outline different types of bankruptcy that individuals and businesses can file for in the United States.

Filing for Bankruptcy:

Petition: To initiate bankruptcy, you must file a petition with the bankruptcy court. You'll also need to provide detailed financial information, including your income, assets, debts, and expenses.

Automatic Stay: Once your petition is filed, an automatic stay is enacted, preventing creditors from pursuing collections actions against you.

Assessment: A bankruptcy trustee or court-appointed official will assess your financial situation to determine how your debts will be handled.

Credit Counseling: Before your debts are discharged, you must complete a credit counseling course approved by the U.S. Trustee Program.

Chapter 7 Bankruptcy (Liquidation):

Liquidation: In a Chapter 7 bankruptcy, a bankruptcy trustee is appointed to oversee your case. They will identify non-exempt assets, sell them, and distribute the proceeds to creditors. Most of your unsecured debts will be discharged, meaning you're no longer legally obligated to repay them.

Chapter 13 Bankruptcy (Reorganization):

Repayment Plan: In Chapter 13 bankruptcy, you'll work with the bankruptcy court to create a repayment plan based on your income and expenses. This plan typically prioritizes secured debts like mortgages and car loans.

Regular Payments: Over the plan's duration, you'll make regular payments to a trustee, who will distribute the funds to your creditors.

Debt Discharge: Once you successfully complete the repayment plan, any remaining qualifying unsecured debts are discharged.

Conclusion

In the labyrinthine world of debt relief, bankruptcy stands as a powerful yet complex tool. It offers a fresh start to individuals and businesses burdened by overwhelming debt, providing a legal means to discharge or restructure their financial obligations. However, bankruptcy should be considered thoughtfully, and alternative debt relief solutions explored before taking the plunge.

The decision to file for bankruptcy is a significant one, with profound financial and emotional implications. It's crucial to assess your unique financial situation, weigh the pros and cons, and, if necessary, consult with a bankruptcy attorney or financial advisor. While bankruptcy can offer respite from debt, it also carries consequences, including the impact on your credit score and the potential loss of assets.

Additionally, exploring alternative debt relief options such as debt consolidation, debt management plans, and debt settlement can provide viable alternatives to bankruptcy. These methods may allow you to regain control of your finances without the long-term repercussions associated with bankruptcy.

Ultimately, breaking free from debt requires a thorough understanding of your financial circumstances, a carefully considered strategy, and, in some cases, professional guidance. Whether you choose bankruptcy or an alternative debt relief solution, the goal is the same: to move toward a future free from the suffocating weight of debt. By making informed decisions and taking proactive steps, you can pave the way for a more secure and financially stable future.

Chapter 10. Debt Prevention and Financial Planning

Introduction

Debt can be a relentless and unforgiving burden that weighs down individuals and families alike. It can limit your financial freedom, hinder your ability to achieve your dreams, and cause persistent stress. Breaking free from debt is a journey that requires both determination and strategy. One crucial aspect of this journey is debt prevention through effective financial planning. In this article, we will explore key strategies for avoiding future debt and setting yourself on a path towards financial security and success.

Tips for Avoiding Future Debt

1. Budgeting: The Foundation of Financial Health

The cornerstone of debt prevention is creating and sticking to a budget. A well-structured budget allows you to track your income and expenses, ensuring that you live within your means. Begin by listing all your sources of income, including your salary, rental income, or any other sources. Next, categorize your expenses into fixed (e.g., mortgage or rent) and variable (e.g., groceries, entertainment). Ensure that your expenses do not exceed your income. A budget acts as a roadmap, helping you make informed financial decisions and avoid impulse spending.

2. Live Below Your Means

Living within your means is a fundamental principle of debt prevention. It involves making choices that prioritize savings and financial security over immediate gratification. This might mean opting for a smaller home or less expensive car than you can afford, or cooking meals at home instead of dining out regularly. The money you save can be used to build an emergency fund and invest in your future, rather than accumulating debt.

3. Reduce and Eliminate High-Interest Debt

If you currently have high-interest debts, such as credit card balances, prioritize paying them off as soon as possible. High-interest debt can quickly spiral out of control and become a significant financial burden. Consider using the snowball or avalanche method to tackle your debts systematically. The snowball method involves paying off the smallest debts first, while the avalanche method focuses on the highest interest rate debts. Whichever method you choose, make consistent, extra payments towards your debts until they are fully paid off.

4. Use Credit Wisely

Credit cards and loans can be valuable financial tools when used responsibly. However, they can also lead to debt if not managed wisely. To prevent future debt, use credit cards for convenience, not as a source of financing. Pay your credit card balances in full each month to avoid interest charges. Additionally, be cautious when taking out loans, and only borrow when it's absolutely necessary and you have a clear plan for repayment.

Setting Financial Goals

1. Define Your Financial Objectives

Setting clear financial goals is an essential step in debt prevention. Your goals give you a sense of purpose and direction, motivating you to make sound financial decisions. Start by defining both short-term and long-term goals. Short-term goals might include paying off credit card debt or saving for a vacation, while long-term goals could involve retirement planning, homeownership, or funding your children's education.

2. Prioritize Your Goals

Not all financial goals are equal in terms of urgency and importance. Prioritize your goals based on their significance and time sensitivity. Emergency savings and debt reduction should generally take precedence over other objectives because they provide financial security and reduce the risk of accumulating more debt.

3. Create a Realistic Plan

After identifying and prioritizing your goals, develop a detailed plan to achieve them. Break down larger goals into smaller, manageable steps. For example, if your goal is to save for a down payment on a house, outline how much you need to save each month and identify areas in your budget where you can cut back to allocate more funds towards your goal.

Building an Emergency Fund

1. The Importance of an Emergency Fund

An emergency fund is your financial safety net. It provides a buffer against unexpected expenses, such as medical bills, car repairs, or job loss, that can otherwise lead to debt. Without an emergency fund, you may be forced to rely on credit cards or loans when emergencies arise, exacerbating your financial troubles.

2. How Much to Save

The size of your emergency fund depends on your individual circumstances, but a common rule of thumb is to aim for three to six months' worth of living expenses. Calculate your monthly expenses, including rent or mortgage, utilities, groceries, insurance, and transportation, and multiply this by the number of months you want to cover.

3. Start Small and Be Consistent

Building an emergency fund doesn't have to happen overnight. Start by setting aside a small portion of your income regularly, even if it's just a few dollars each week. Over time, increase the amount as your financial situation improves. Automate your savings by setting up automatic transfers from your checking account to your savings account to ensure consistency.

4. Use Windfalls and Bonuses Wisely

Windfalls, such as tax refunds or work bonuses, provide an excellent opportunity to boost your emergency fund. Instead of splurging on non-essential purchases, consider allocating a significant portion of windfalls towards your emergency fund. This will help you reach your goal faster and provide added peace of mind.

Conclusion

Debt prevention and financial planning are intertwined, serving as vital tools for achieving and maintaining financial security. By following the tips for avoiding future debt, setting clear financial goals, and building an emergency fund, you can proactively protect yourself from the pitfalls of debt.

Remember that financial success is not a destination but a journey that requires continuous effort and discipline. Regularly review your budget, adjust your goals as circumstances change, and stay committed to living within your means. With dedication and smart financial planning, you can break free from debt and build a future of financial stability and prosperity.

Introduction

Debt is a pervasive part of modern life, and for many, it can be a double-edged sword. On one hand, it can provide opportunities for growth and financial stability, enabling us to purchase homes, pursue education, or start businesses. However, debt also has a darker side, one that often lurks in the shadows: debt-related stress. The burden of debt can take a significant emotional toll on individuals and families, affecting their mental health, relationships, and overall well-being. In this article, we will explore the emotional toll of debt, coping strategies to manage debt-related stress, the importance of seeking professional help, and ultimately, how to break free from the shackles of debt-related stress.

The Emotional Toll of Debt

1. Anxiety and Worry

Debt can bring about relentless anxiety and worry. Concerns about making monthly payments, meeting interest obligations, and dealing with creditors can keep you up at night, leaving you physically and emotionally drained. The constant fear of financial instability can lead to sleepless nights, increased heart rate, and a pervasive sense of dread.

2. Depression and Low Self-Esteem

Living under the weight of debt can lead to feelings of hopelessness and worthlessness. Debt-related stress can contribute to depression, as individuals grapple with feelings of inadequacy, guilt, and self-blame. When you can't keep up with your financial commitments, it's easy to internalize failure and lose confidence in your ability to manage your life.

3. Strained Relationships

Money matters are a common source of conflict in relationships. Debt-related stress can strain even the strongest bonds, leading to arguments, resentment, and a breakdown in communication. It's not uncommon for couples to blame each other for their financial predicament, further exacerbating their emotional distress.

4. Isolation and Shame

Debt-related stress can make you withdraw from social activities and isolate yourself from friends and family. The shame associated with financial difficulties can be paralyzing, causing individuals to hide their struggles and avoid seeking support. This isolation can further exacerbate the emotional toll of debt.

Coping Strategies

1. Face the Reality

The first step in dealing with debt-related stress is to confront the reality of your financial situation. Create a detailed inventory of your debts, including the amounts, interest rates, and payment schedules. Understanding the scope of your debt is essential for devising a plan to tackle it.

2. Budgeting and Financial Planning

Develop a realistic budget that allows you to allocate funds for debt repayment while covering essential expenses. A well-thought-out budget can help you regain a sense of control over your finances. Consider consulting with a financial advisor to create a strategic debt repayment plan.

3. Prioritize Debts

Not all debts are created equal. Prioritize high-interest debts, such as credit card balances, as they can quickly spiral out of control. Make minimum payments on lower-interest debts while directing extra funds toward high-interest ones. As you pay off high-interest debts, you'll feel a sense of accomplishment and reduced stress.

4. Open Communication

If you're in a relationship, open and honest communication with your partner is crucial. Discuss your financial situation, goals, and concerns openly. Together, you can develop a joint strategy for managing and reducing your debt. Remember that you're a team, and tackling debt is a shared responsibility.

5. Seek Emotional Support

Don't underestimate the power of emotional support from friends and family. Share your struggles with trusted individuals who can offer a listening ear, empathy, and encouragement. Bottling up your emotions will only intensify the stress.

6. Mindfulness and Stress Reduction Techniques

Incorporate mindfulness practices, meditation, or deep breathing exercises into your daily routine to manage stress. These techniques can help you stay grounded and reduce anxiety. Regular exercise and a healthy diet can also have a positive impact on your emotional well-being.

Seeking Professional Help

1. Credit Counseling

Credit counseling agencies can provide valuable assistance in managing debt-related stress. They offer financial education, budgeting advice, and debt management plans tailored to your unique situation. These plans often involve negotiating with creditors to reduce interest rates or create more manageable repayment terms.

2. Debt Consolidation

Debt consolidation involves taking out a single loan to pay off multiple debts. This can simplify your monthly payments and potentially lower your overall interest rate. However, it's essential to explore this option carefully and understand the terms and fees associated with consolidation.

3. Bankruptcy

Bankruptcy should be considered as a last resort when all other options have been exhausted. While it can provide relief from overwhelming debt, it also comes with long-term financial consequences. Consult with a bankruptcy attorney to understand the implications and determine if it's the right choice for your situation.

4. Therapy and Counseling

Debt-related stress can be emotionally taxing, and seeking therapy or counseling can be incredibly beneficial. Therapists can help you develop coping strategies, address underlying emotional issues, and work on rebuilding your self-esteem. Couples therapy can also assist in improving communication and resolving relationship conflicts related to debt. Couples therapy, also known as marriage or relationship therapy, is a form of counseling that helps couples address and resolve conflicts, improve communication, and work on relationship issues with the guidance of a trained therapist.

5. Legal Advice

In cases where debt collectors are engaging in harassing or unfair practices, it may be necessary to seek legal advice. An attorney specializing in consumer rights can help protect your interests and ensure your rights are upheld under the law.

Conclusion

Dealing with debt-related stress is a journey that requires resilience, patience, and determination. It's essential to acknowledge the emotional toll that debt can take on your mental health and relationships. By facing the reality of your financial situation, creating a strategic plan, and seeking support from professionals and loved ones, you can take proactive steps toward regaining control of your life.

Remember that you are not alone in your struggle with debt-related stress. There are resources and strategies available to help you break free from its grip. By taking decisive action and prioritizing your emotional well-being, you can pave the way toward a brighter financial future, free from the suffocating burden of debt-related stress.

Introduction

Debt is a pervasive and often burdensome aspect of modern life. Whether it's student loans, credit card debt, mortgages, or medical bills, debt can quickly accumulate and become overwhelming. However, it's important to remember that financial freedom is attainable, and there are inspiring stories of individuals who have successfully conquered their debts. In this article, we will delve into real-life case studies and success stories of people who have broken free from debt's clutches. These stories not only serve as a source of motivation but also offer valuable lessons and strategies for anyone seeking to regain control of their financial lives.

Real-Life Examples of Debt Management

1. The Student Loan Redemption: Emma's Story

Emma graduated from a prestigious university with a mountain of student loan debt. She faced the daunting task of repaying tens of thousands of dollars while still managing her day-to-day expenses. Emma's journey to debt freedom was a meticulous one. She started by creating a comprehensive budget, cutting unnecessary expenses, and redirecting those savings towards her student loan payments. She also explored income-driven repayment options, which helped lower her monthly obligations. Through discipline, determination, and a side gig, Emma chipped away at her student loan debt faster than she had ever imagined. Her perseverance paid off, and she is now debt-free, enjoying the financial freedom she once thought was unattainable.

2. Credit Card Comeback: Mark's Triumph

Mark found himself ensnared in a web of credit card debt. He was living paycheck to paycheck, barely making minimum payments, and constantly stressed about his financial situation. Recognizing that something had to change, Mark devised a debt repayment plan. He consolidated his credit card balances into a lower-interest loan, reducing his overall interest burden. He then negotiated with creditors to lower his interest rates further and began paying more than the minimum required. Mark also explored balance transfer offers to accelerate his debt reduction. Balance transfer offers refer to promotional deals provided by credit card issuers that allow cardholders to transfer existing credit card debt from one card to another with lower or even zero interest rates for a specified period, helping individuals save on interest and manage their debt more effectively. It took time and discipline, but Mark successfully paid off his credit card debt. Today, he enjoys a debt-free life and is building a secure financial future.

3. Mortgage Miracle: The Smith Family

The Smith family faced a unique challenge when their adjustable-rate mortgage began to spiral out of control. Rising interest rates had pushed their monthly mortgage payments beyond their means, and foreclosure loomed ominously. In a desperate bid to save their home, they worked tirelessly to refinance their mortgage at a fixed rate. This not only stabilized their monthly payments but also allowed them to negotiate more favorable terms. By living frugally and redirecting extra income towards their mortgage, the Smiths managed to pay off their loan years ahead of schedule. They now own their home outright and have not only avoided foreclosure but also created a valuable asset for their family's future.

4. The Power of Financial Education: Sarah's Story

Sarah grew up in a family where financial literacy was a priority. Armed with this knowledge, she entered adulthood with a strong foundation but still found herself in a significant amount of debt after college. Instead of panicking, Sarah applied the principles she had learned. She tackled her debt strategically, focusing on high-interest loans first. She also took advantage of balance transfer offers and diligently tracked her spending. Sarah's dedication to financial education paid off, and she became debt-free within a few years. Today, she actively shares her knowledge through financial literacy workshops, empowering others to break free from debt's shackles.

5. The Support System: John and Maria's Journey

John and Maria faced a unique challenge as a couple managing their finances. They had accumulated substantial credit card debt, and their relationship was strained by financial stress. However, they decided to face their debt problem together. They attended financial counseling sessions, created a joint budget, and committed to open communication about their finances. With a shared goal and a strong support system, John and Maria were able to make significant progress in paying off their debt. They even started a side business together, which provided extra income to accelerate their debt repayment. Their journey not only resulted in a debt-free life but also strengthened their relationship.

David's debt story began with a failed business venture that left him with both personal and business debts. Rather than succumbing to despair, he used his entrepreneurial spirit to turn his life around. David started a new business, focusing on his passion and market demand. The income from his new venture was directed toward paying off his debts. It wasn't easy, but David's determination paid off as his business grew. Within a few years, he had not only paid off his debts but also achieved financial success. Today, he attributes his financial triumph to resilience and the ability to turn setbacks into opportunities.

Conclusion

These case studies and success stories demonstrate that breaking free from debt is achievable with the right mindset, strategies, and support. Whether you are burdened by student loans, credit card debt, or a mortgage, there is hope. By taking control of your finances, creating a budget, exploring debt consolidation options, and seeking financial education, you can pave the way to a debt-free future.

These stories also underscore the importance of perseverance, discipline, and a willingness to adapt. Financial setbacks can happen to anyone, but they do not have to define your financial future. With determination and a well-thought-out plan, you can conquer your debts and create a more secure financial foundation for yourself and your family.

In the end, these real-life examples serve as beacons of hope and inspiration for those facing the challenges of debt. They remind us that with the right strategies and mindset, anyone can break free from debt's grip and build a brighter financial future. So, take the lessons from these stories, apply them to your own situation, and embark on your journey toward financial freedom. Your debt-free future is waiting.

Introduction

Debt is a ubiquitous aspect of modern life. Most individuals and businesses have at some point found themselves dealing with debt, whether it's in the form of loans, credit card balances, mortgages, or other financial obligations. While taking on debt is sometimes necessary to achieve specific goals or maintain financial stability, it can also be a source of stress and anxiety. Understanding the legal aspects of debt is crucial for anyone looking to manage their financial well-being effectively.

In this article, we will delve into the legal aspects of debt, examining important factors such as debt collection laws, consumer rights and protections, and how to avoid falling victim to debt scams. By gaining a comprehensive understanding of these legal aspects, individuals and businesses can make informed decisions about their finances and navigate the complex world of debt more effectively.

Debt Collection Laws

Debt collection is a multi-billion-dollar industry that involves creditors and third-party debt collectors attempting to recover outstanding debts from individuals and businesses. To prevent abusive and unfair practices in the debt collection process, various laws have been enacted at both the federal and state levels. Understanding these laws is essential for individuals and businesses dealing with debt collection agencies.

FDCPA, which stands for the Fair Debt Collection Practices Act, pertains to the United States. It is a federal law in the United States that regulates the practices of third-party debt collectors and aims to protect consumers from abusive and unfair debt collection practices. It applies to third-party debt collectors, not creditors collecting their own debts. Under the FDCPA, debt collectors are prohibited from engaging in abusive, deceptive, or unfair practices. Some key provisions of the FDCPA include:

- Debt collectors must identify themselves and disclose the purpose of their communication.
- They cannot contact debtors at inconvenient times or places, such as before 8 a.m. or after 9 p.m.
- Harassment, threats, or false statements by debt collectors are strictly prohibited.
- Debtors have the right to dispute the debt and request validation within 30 days of being contacted.
- Debt collectors must cease communication if the debtor requests it in writing.

2. State Debt Collection Laws

In addition to federal laws like the FDCPA, individual states have their own debt collection laws. These laws may provide additional protections and regulations that debt collectors must adhere to. It's crucial to be aware of both federal and state laws when dealing with debt collection agencies.

Consumer Rights and Protections

Individuals who find themselves in debt have several rights and protections under the law to ensure fair treatment and opportunities for debt relief. Understanding these rights can help individuals make informed decisions when dealing with creditors or considering debt management options.

1. Right to Accurate Credit Reporting

The Fair Credit Reporting Act (FCRA) is a U.S. federal law that regulates the collection, accuracy, and use of consumer credit information, ensuring the fair and accurate reporting of individuals' credit histories. It ensures that consumers have the right to accurate and fair credit reporting. This means that creditors and credit reporting agencies must provide accurate information about an individual's credit history. Consumers have the right to dispute inaccurate information on their credit reports.

2. Bankruptcy Protections

Bankruptcy is a legal process that allows individuals and businesses to discharge or restructure their debts when they are unable to pay them. In the United States, the two primary types of bankruptcy for individuals are Chapter 7 and Chapter 13. Bankruptcy provides a fresh start for those overwhelmed by debt and offers protection from creditor harassment, wage garnishments, and foreclosure.

3. Debt Relief Options

Beyond bankruptcy, there are various debt relief options available to individuals, such as debt consolidation, debt settlement, and credit counseling. These options can provide a structured way to manage and reduce debt, but individuals should be cautious and research thoroughly before committing to any debt relief program to avoid scams.

Avoiding Debt Scams

Unfortunately, the world of debt also attracts scammers who prey on individuals struggling with financial difficulties. Being aware of common debt scams and knowing how to protect oneself is vital.

1. Advance Fee Scams

In these scams, individuals are promised debt relief or a loan in exchange for an upfront fee. Legitimate debt relief programs do not require payment before providing services. Always be skeptical of any request for upfront fees.

2. Phantom Debt Scams

Phantom debt scammers claim that individuals owe debts that may not even exist. They often use aggressive tactics, such as threats of legal action or arrest, to intimidate victims into paying. Always verify the legitimacy of a debt before making payments.

3. Identity Theft and Fraud

Identity theft can lead to fraudulent debts in your name. Protect your personal information and regularly monitor your credit reports for any suspicious activity. If you suspect identity theft, report it immediately.

4. Debt Settlement Scams

Some debt settlement companies promise to negotiate with creditors to reduce your debt but fail to deliver on their promises. Before enrolling in a debt settlement program, research the company thoroughly and consider alternatives.

Conclusion

Dealing with debt is a reality for many individuals and businesses. However, understanding the legal aspects of debt is essential for managing it effectively and avoiding potential pitfalls. Debt collection laws, consumer rights, and protections, as well as knowledge about how to avoid debt scams, are critical components of financial literacy.

In the United States, by familiarizing themselves with the Fair Debt Collection Practices Act (FDCPA), consumers can ensure that debt collectors treat them fairly and avoid abusive practices. Additionally, knowing their rights under the Fair Credit Reporting Act (FCRA) and the options available, including bankruptcy and debt relief programs, empowers individuals to make informed decisions about their financial future. Consumers of other countries should refer to the relevant acts applicable in their own country for similar protections.

In the digital age, where scams abound, vigilance is key. Recognizing common debt scams and being cautious of any requests for upfront fees or threats of legal action can protect individuals from falling victim to fraudulent schemes. It's also essential to safeguard personal information to prevent identity theft and fraudulent debts.

In conclusion, breaking free from debt requires both financial discipline and a comprehensive understanding of the legal aspects surrounding debt. Armed with knowledge and awareness, individuals and businesses can navigate the complex world of debt with confidence and work towards achieving financial freedom.

Introduction

Breaking free from debt is a monumental achievement in one's financial journey. It signifies a turning point where individuals can shift their focus from managing liabilities to accumulating assets and building wealth. One of the most effective ways to embark on this journey is through smart and strategic investing. This article will guide you through the transition from debt to wealth and provide essential investment strategies and long-term financial planning tips to help you secure your financial future.

Transitioning from Debt to Wealth

The road from debt to wealth is a transformative journey that requires a combination of discipline, knowledge, and patience. Here are some critical steps to make this transition:

Debt Elimination: Before you can start building wealth, it's crucial to eliminate high-interest debt. This includes credit card debt, personal loans, and any other high-cost liabilities. The interest you pay on these debts can erode your wealth-building potential.

Emergency Fund: Build a robust emergency fund to cover unexpected expenses. Having this financial safety net will prevent you from falling back into debt when unexpected costs arise.

Budgeting and Financial Discipline: Implement a budget and stick to it. This will help you manage your spending, live within your means, and have money available for investing.

Increase Income: Look for opportunities to increase your income, such as taking on a side job or improving your skills to advance your career. The more money you have available to invest, the faster you can build wealth.

Education: Invest in financial education. Understanding different investment options, risk management, and long-term financial planning is essential for success in wealth building.

Investment Strategies for the Debt-Free

Once you've cleared your debts and established a strong financial foundation, it's time to explore various investment strategies to grow your wealth. Here are some effective approaches:

Stock Market Investing: Investing in individual stocks or exchange-traded funds (ETFs) can provide significant long-term returns. Diversify your portfolio across different industries and sectors to spread risk. Consider both growth and dividend-paying stocks based on your risk tolerance and goals.

Real Estate: Real estate can be an excellent investment, offering both income potential and property appreciation. You can invest directly in properties, participate in real estate investment trusts (REITs), or explore crowdfunding platforms for real estate projects.

A REIT, or Real Estate Investment Trust, is a company that owns, operates, or finances income-producing real estate properties and offers investors the opportunity to invest in a diversified real estate portfolio. Crowdfunding platforms are online platforms that enable individuals, businesses, or organizations to raise funds from a large number of people, typically through small contributions from a diverse group of investors or donors.

Retirement Accounts: Maximize your contributions to tax-advantaged retirement accounts like a 401(k) or an IRA (applicable to United States). These accounts offer tax benefits and can help you secure your financial future. Choose investments within these accounts that align with your long-term goals.

Diversification: Diversify your investments across asset classes, including stocks, bonds, and alternative investments like precious metals or cryptocurrencies. Diversification helps reduce risk and ensures your portfolio remains resilient in various market conditions.

Dollar-Cost Averaging: Implement a dollar-cost averaging strategy, where you invest a fixed amount of money at regular intervals, regardless of market conditions. This strategy minimizes the impact of market volatility and allows you to buy more shares when prices are low.

Seek Professional Guidance: Consider consulting a financial advisor or investment professional to develop a personalized investment strategy tailored to your financial goals, risk tolerance, and time horizon.

Long-Term Financial Planning

Building wealth isn't just about making investment choices; it's also about long-term financial planning. Here are essential considerations to ensure your financial success over the years:

Set Clear Goals: **Define your financial goals, both short-term and long-term. These goals will serve as a roadmap for your financial planning efforts.**

Create a Budget: **Continue to maintain a budget that reflects your current financial situation and goals. Regularly review and adjust it as needed.**

Emergency Fund Maintenance: **Keep your emergency fund adequately funded. Life is full of surprises, and having a financial cushion will prevent you from dipping into your investments during emergencies.**

Insurance Coverage: **Ensure you have adequate insurance coverage, including health, life, and property insurance. Insurance can protect your assets and provide peace of mind.**

Estate Planning: **Develop an estate plan that outlines how your assets will be distributed after your passing. This includes creating a will, designating beneficiaries, and possibly setting up trusts.**

Tax Efficiency: **Stay informed about tax laws and consider tax-efficient investment strategies. Reducing your tax liability can significantly impact your long-term wealth.**

Regular Monitoring: **Continuously monitor your investments and financial plan. Make adjustments as needed to stay on track with your goals and adapt to changing circumstances.**

Educate Yourself: **Keep learning about personal finance and investing. The financial landscape evolves, and staying informed will help you make informed decisions.**

Conclusion

Breaking free from debt and building wealth is a commendable achievement that requires dedication and strategic planning. It's a journey that transitions individuals from a state of financial vulnerability to one of financial security and abundance. By following the steps outlined in this article, you can navigate this transition successfully.

Remember, investing is a powerful tool on this journey, but it should be approached with careful consideration of your goals, risk tolerance, and financial situation. Diversify your investments, seek professional advice when needed, and stay committed to your long-term financial plan. With time, patience, and perseverance, you can break free from debt and secure a prosperous financial future.

"Breaking Free from Debt" is a comprehensive guide that offers readers a transformative journey towards financial freedom. Starting with an exploration of debt management, it defines debt, underscores its importance, and highlights common types of debt. Readers are then guided to assess their financial health, create personal budgets, and track expenses. The book helps readers differentiate between good and bad debt, providing strategies for minimizing the latter. It covers various types of debt, from credit cards to student loans, and offers insights into debt consolidation and refinancing.

Practical debt repayment methods, negotiation skills with creditors, and credit score improvement techniques are all part of this invaluable resource. The emotional toll of debt and strategies to cope with it are addressed, along with legal aspects, investment opportunities, and long-term wealth-building strategies. Real-life case studies and success stories inspire and motivate readers on their path to financial recovery and prosperity. "Breaking Free from Debt" is your roadmap to a debt-free and financially secure future.

ABOUT THE AUTHOR

Mr. C. P. Kumar is a retired Scientist 'G' from National Institute of Hydrology, Roorkee, Uttarakhand, India. He is also a Reiki Healer and Chakra Balancing practitioner (with pendulum dowsing) and offers Emotional Freedom Technique (EFT) to help individuals with emotional issues. Mr. Kumar has authored many books on technical, spiritual, and social topics.

For further details, you may visit his webpage
https://www.angelfire.com/nh/cpkumar/virgo.html